THE 9/11 TERRORIST ATTACKS

Nick Rebman

Apex is distributed by North Star Editions:
sales@northstareditions.com | 888-417-0195

Produced for Apex by Red Line Editorial.

Photographs ©: Moshe Bursuker/AP Images, cover, 1; David Karp/AP Images, 4–5; Spencer Platt/Getty Images News/Getty Images, 6–7; Robert Nickelsberg/Hulton Archive/Getty Images, 8–9; Peter Turnley/VCG/Corbis Historical/Getty Images, 10–11; Nasser Shiyoukhi/AP Images, 12–13; Getty Images News/Getty Images, 14–15; Shutterstock Images, 16–17, 32–33, 38–39, 52–53, 56–57; US Navy/Getty Images News/Getty Images, 18–19; Carol M. Highsmith/Library of Congress, 20–21; Ernesto Mora/ AP Images, 22–23; Thomas Nilsson/Getty Images News/Getty Images, 24–25; Don Halasy/Library of Congress, 26–27; National Archives, 28–29, 30–31; Joshua Gunter/The Plain Dealer/AP Images, 34–35; Paul Morse/ George W. Bush Presidential Library/Donaldson Collection/Michael Ochs Archives/Getty Images, 37; Preston Keres/US Navy/Getty Images News/ Getty Images, 40–41; Andrea Booher/FEMA/Getty Images News/Getty Images, 42–43; Fritz Reiss/AP Images, 44–45; Library of Congress, 47, 58; Karla Ann Coté/Sipa USA/AP Images, 48–49; Paula Bronstein/Getty Images News/Getty Images, 50–51; Stan Honda/AFP/Getty Images, 54–55

Library of Congress Control Number: 2024942355

ISBN
979-8-89250-460-7 (hardcover)
979-8-89250-476-8 (paperback)
979-8-89250-506-2 (ebook pdf)
979-8-89250-492-8 (hosted ebook)

Printed in the United States of America
Mankato, MN
012025

NOTE TO PARENTS AND EDUCATORS

Apex books are designed to build literacy skills in striving readers. Exciting, high-interest content attracts and holds readers' attention. The text is carefully leveled to allow students to achieve success quickly.

TABLE OF CONTENTS

Chapter 1

A DAY OF TERROR

September 11, 2001, began as a normal Tuesday morning. In New York City, the sky was blue. People went to work. But at 8:46 a.m., everything changed. An airplane crashed into the North Tower of the World Trade Center. Hundreds of people died instantly.

The North Tower of the World Trade Center burns after being hit by a plane on September 11, 2001.

An explosion rocks the South Tower (left) on September 11.

The crash caused a huge explosion. Smoke and flames spewed out of the building. Firefighters rushed to the scene. Then, at 9:03 a.m., another airplane arrived. It crashed into the South Tower. The United States was under attack.

WORLD TRADE CENTER

The World Trade Center was a set of office buildings. The two tallest buildings were known as the Twin Towers. They opened in the early 1970s. At that time, they were the tallest buildings in the world. Each tower stood 110 stories tall.

Chapter 2

AL-QAEDA FORMS

A group called al-Qaeda carried out the 9/11 attacks. Al-Qaeda is an Islamic militant group. It does not want non-Muslim countries to interfere with Muslim nations. In 1979, the Soviet Union invaded Afghanistan. The Soviet Union was a non-Muslim country. Most people in Afghanistan were Muslims. So, al-Qaeda formed in the late 1980s. It helped the Muslim fighters during this war.

Afghan fighters defeated the Soviet Union in 1989.

US soldiers train in Saudi Arabia for the Persian Gulf War in 1990.

The Persian Gulf War took place from 1990 to 1991. A large group of countries fought against Iraq. The United States led the group. During this war, the king of Saudi Arabia let US forces stay in his country. Saudi Arabia is a Muslim country. Al-Qaeda saw the US soldiers as invaders.

HOLY CITIES

Islam started in the 600s. The religion began in Saudi Arabia. This country is home to two of Islam's most important cities. One is Mecca. The other is Medina. Muslims consider these cities holy.

Al-Qaeda opposed the United States for other reasons, too. For example, the United States has supported Israel for many years. Israel invaded Palestine in 1967. Most people in Palestine are Muslims. Since then, many Palestinian people have suffered under Israeli rule.

AL-QAEDA AND ISLAM

There are more than 1.8 billion Muslims in the world. Nearly all of them oppose violence. In fact, the word *Islam* comes from a word meaning "peace." However, al-Qaeda believes in an extreme form of Islam. It supports the use of terrorism. That is when people use violence to reach their goals.

Israeli soldiers force Palestinians to go through security checks. This makes it hard for Palestinians to do everyday tasks.

Osama bin Laden was born in 1957 in Saudi Arabia.

Osama bin Laden was the leader of al-Qaeda. In 1996, he called for a war against the United States. Afghanistan's leaders supported bin Laden. They let him set up camps in their country. Al-Qaeda fighters trained for war.

BOMBINGS IN AFRICA

In 1998, al-Qaeda carried out two bombings. Both hit US government buildings in East Africa. The bombings killed more than 200 people. Thousands more were hurt. Some al-Qaeda members were arrested. But others got away.

In 1999, al-Qaeda started planning a major attack. Over the next two years, 19 members of the group entered the United States. Some of them learned how to fly planes. Some knew about the plans as they developed. Others knew little until September 11, 2001.

Some members of al-Qaeda got pilot training in Venice, Florida.

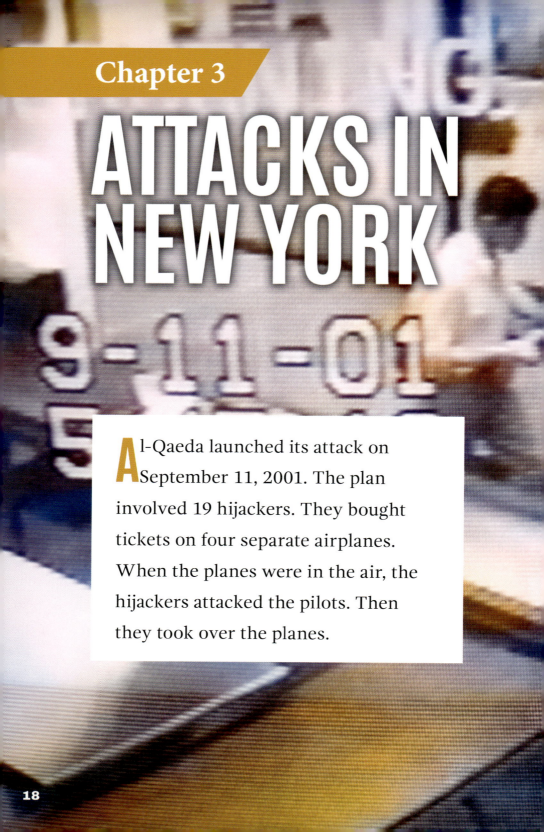

Chapter 3

ATTACKS IN NEW YORK

Al-Qaeda launched its attack on September 11, 2001. The plan involved 19 hijackers. They bought tickets on four separate airplanes. When the planes were in the air, the hijackers attacked the pilots. Then they took over the planes.

Two of the hijackers go through airport security on the morning of September 11, 2001.

The hijackers flew the first plane to New York City. They crashed the plane into the North Tower of the World Trade Center. At first, most people thought it was an accident. No one knew another plane was coming.

SYMBOLIC TARGETS

Al-Qaeda was not strong enough to attack the US military. So, the group chose symbolic targets. The World Trade Center stood for US businesses. US businesses have a huge effect on other countries. Al-Qaeda did not approve of this Western influence.

Hundreds of companies had offices in the World Trade Center.

People in New York watch the Twin Towers burn on September 11.

Just 17 minutes later, hijackers crashed the second plane into the South Tower. People realized that the first crash had not been an accident. It was an attack.

FULL OF FUEL

All four planes took off in the eastern United States. And all four were headed to California. That meant the planes had to cross the entire United States. So, they carried lots of fuel. This fuel caused huge explosions when the planes crashed.

The Twin Towers burned. People on the lower floors ran to safety. But people on the upper floors were trapped inside. At 9:59 a.m., the South Tower collapsed. The North Tower collapsed 29 minutes later. Huge clouds of dust rushed through the city.

TOWER 7

Burning rubble fell onto another nearby building. This building was called Tower 7. The burning rubble caused fires to spread. The fires burned for hours. Later that evening, Tower 7 collapsed. By that time, everyone had escaped the building.

The collapse of the
Twin Towers caused
even more destruction.

New York's mayor told people to leave the area if they could. The US government took action, too. Throughout the country, all planes were ordered to land. Also, no planes were allowed to take off.

AIR TRAFFIC CONTROL

More than 4,500 US planes were in the air when the 9/11 attacks happened. More than one million people were on those flights. Air traffic controllers had a massive job. They helped each plane land as soon as possible. More than 700 planes landed within minutes. The rest landed in just a few hours.

People help an injured person on September 11.

Chapter 4

WASHINGTON AND PENNSYLVANIA

The hijackers flew the third plane toward Washington, DC. They crashed the plane into the Pentagon. This target was also symbolic. The Pentagon is the main office of the US military.

The Pentagon burns after being hit by a plane on September 11.

It took $500 million to rebuild the Pentagon.

The crash caused fires in the Pentagon. Parts of the building filled with smoke. Many people ran outside. Others jumped out of windows to safety. But some did not make it. They were trapped inside.

EMPTY OFFICES

Parts of the Pentagon were being fixed. So, the building did not have as many workers there as usual. The plane hit an area that usually had 4,500 people inside. But on September 11, there were only about 800 people in that area.

The hijackers flew the fourth plane toward Washington, DC, too. They wanted to strike the US Capitol. This building is where lawmakers meet. However, the fourth plane took off 25 minutes behind schedule. So, the passengers found out about the other attacks.

PHONE CALLS

Many people didn't have cell phones in 2001. But some planes had phones on them. After the hijackers took over, passengers on the fourth plane used these phones. They called family members. That was how they learned about the other attacks.

The fourth plane took off from an airport in Newark, New Jersey.

Workers clean up the crash site from the fourth plane in Pennsylvania.

The passengers decided to fight back. A group rushed the cockpit. There was a big struggle. The hijackers did not want the passengers to gain control. So, they crashed the plane into a field in Pennsylvania. Everyone on board died. But the passengers saved many other people.

HEROES OF FLIGHT 93

The fourth plane was called Flight 93. Many people said its crew and passengers were heroes. And in 2014, all 40 people on the flight were recognized. They received Congressional Gold Medals. That is Congress's highest non-military honor.

THE PRESIDENT SPEAKS

After the attacks, Americans were in shock. They could hardly believe what had happened. That night, President George W. Bush gave a speech. Many people watched on TV. Bush said Americans were sad. And they were angry. But he said they would stay strong. They would help the people who had been hurt.

Bush also said US forces would find the people who planned the attacks. He stated that there would be a "war against terrorism." This idea became the main focus of his time in office.

In the weeks after 9/11, more than 90 percent of Americans approved of President Bush.

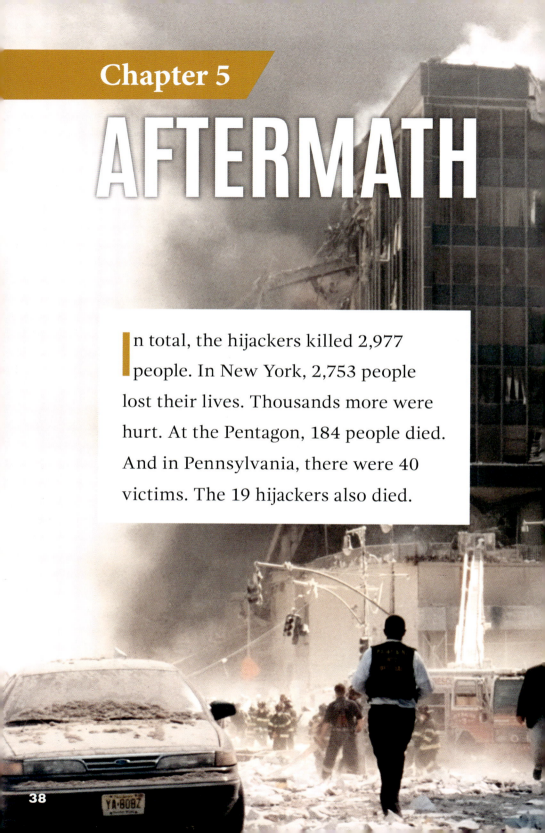

AFTERMATH

In total, the hijackers killed 2,977 people. In New York, 2,753 people lost their lives. Thousands more were hurt. At the Pentagon, 184 people died. And in Pennsylvania, there were 40 victims. The 19 hijackers also died.

The attacks on the Twin Towers left more than 1.2 million tons (1.1 million metric tons) of rubble.

The spot where
the Twin Towers fell
became known as
Ground Zero. First
responders rushed to
the area. Firefighters
and police officers
came. Health-care
workers came. So did
construction workers.
Many others came as
well. First responders
put out fires. They
looked for survivors.
They cleared rubble.
Their work continued
for days.

A firefighter helps with rescue efforts at Ground Zero on September 14, 2001.

People from all over the United States traveled to New York. They helped with the recovery efforts. Other people were not able to go. But they gave blood. They sent supplies. They gave money.

BAD ECONOMY

The 9/11 attacks had a major effect on the US economy. Many businesses suffered. As a result, lots of people lost their jobs. For example, many people were afraid to fly on planes. So, airlines lost money. Less travel caused other impacts. Some places received fewer tourists. Businesses in those places lost money.

Hundreds of search dogs helped look for people at Ground Zero.

People in Germany lay flowers and candles outside a US government building on September 18, 2001.

People around the world showed their support for the United States. Some people sent cards and letters. Others left flowers in front of US government buildings. People also gathered in large groups. They held candles. They hoped for peace.

REBUILDING

Ground Zero took eight months to clean up. People worked day and night. They cleared away the rubble. Then they started to rebuild. A new World Trade Center went up. The building is called One World Trade Center. It opened in 2014.

FIRST RESPONDERS

Thousands of first responders put themselves at risk. They ran into the burning buildings while other people were running out. First responders helped people who were hurt. They helped people get to safety. They saved thousands of lives. Many people said they were heroes.

More than 400 first responders died during the attacks. Hundreds more died in the years that followed. They got sick from all the dust. They had problems breathing.

Being a first responder after 9/11 was very dangerous work.

Chapter 6

LEGACY

After September 11, Islamophobia rose. Some Americans became suspicious of all Muslims. South Asian, Arab, and Middle Eastern people were also targeted. Hate crimes against these groups increased. US law enforcement unfairly targeted them, too.

Protests by Muslim Americans helped bring attention to the problem of Islamophobia after September 11.

Al-Qaeda was based in Afghanistan. That country's government supported al-Qaeda. So, in October 2001, US forces invaded. They removed Afghanistan's government. They also set up a new government. In 2021, US forces left. Afghanistan's old government soon regained power.

WAR IN IRAQ

Iraq had nothing to do with the September 11 attacks. However, President Bush falsely linked the attacks to Iraq. Then, in 2003, Bush ordered an invasion of Iraq. The war lasted eight years. Much of the country was destroyed.

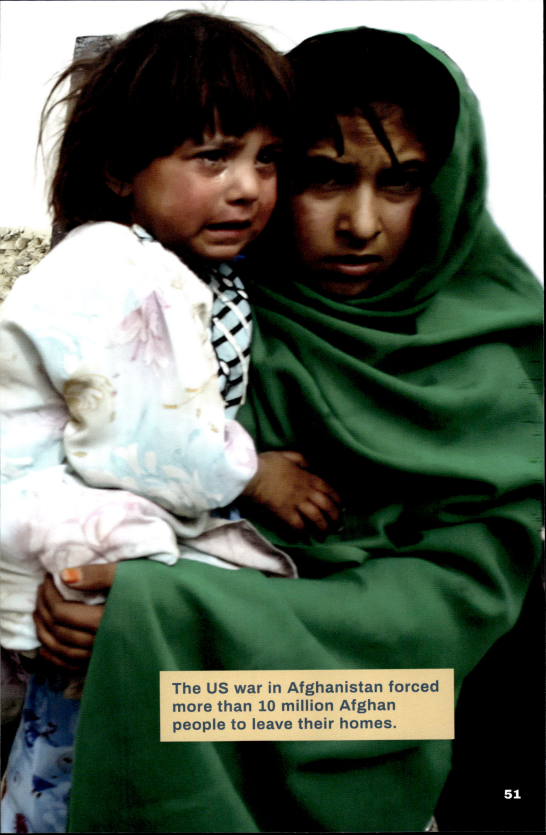

The US war in Afghanistan forced more than 10 million Afghan people to leave their homes.

After 9/11, airports used many more security tools.

In October 2001, President Bush signed a new law. It was called the Patriot Act. The law was supposed to help stop future attacks. But it also helped the US government spy on people. The government no longer needed a warrant to do so. Some people worried. They thought the law took away their privacy.

AIRPORT SECURITY

The 9/11 hijackers used knives to attack the pilots. After the attacks, airport security changed. People could no longer take sharp objects onto planes. The government also created the TSA. This group helps keep airports safe.

There were also health impacts after 9/11. The attacks created huge dust clouds. Survivors breathed in this dust. It led to many health problems. Thousands of people died in the following years. Cancer was one common cause. Many survivors also dealt with trauma and loss.

DEATH OF BIN LADEN

After the attacks, Osama bin Laden stayed in hiding. The US military hunted him for several years. Finally, in 2011, they found him. He was in Pakistan. US forces entered his home. They killed him.

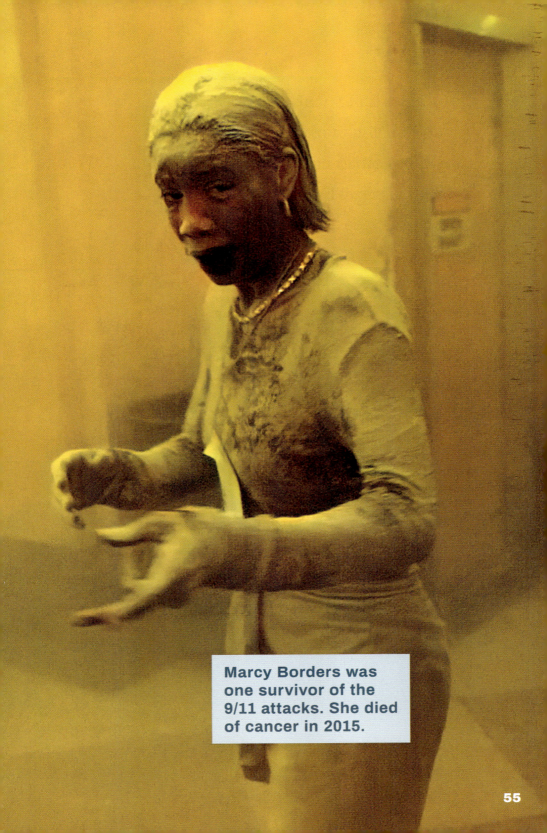

Marcy Borders was one survivor of the 9/11 attacks. She died of cancer in 2015.

In 2011, a memorial opened in New York City. It has two large pools of water. They lie where the Twin Towers stood. The names of the victims are written around the pools' edges. In 2014, a museum opened. There, visitors can learn more about the attacks.

OTHER MEMORIALS

In 2008, a memorial opened in Washington, DC. There are 184 benches. Each one has a victim's name on it. There is a memorial in Pennsylvania, too. People can visit the field where the plane crashed. They can honor the victims.

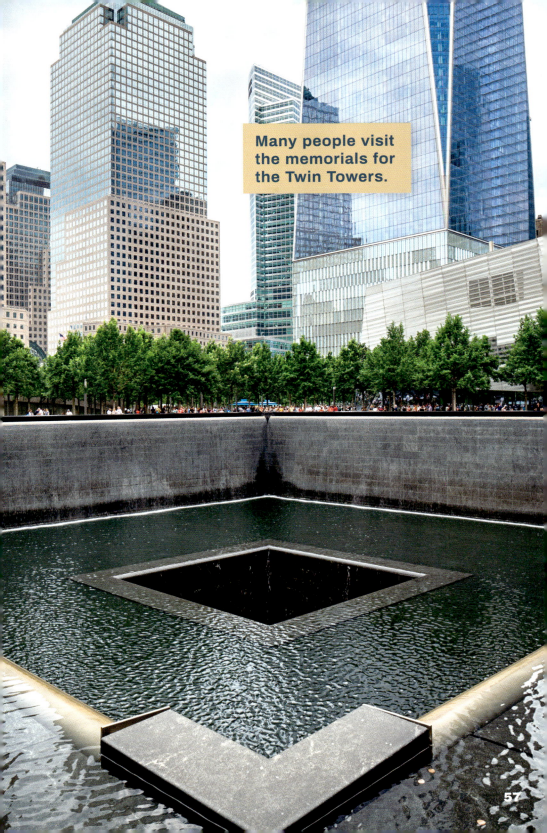

Many people visit the memorials for the Twin Towers.

TIMELINE

SEPTEMBER 11, 2001, 8:46 A.M.	Al-Qaeda hijackers crash a plane into the North Tower of the World Trade Center in New York City.
9:03 A.M.	Al-Qaeda hijackers crash a second plane into the South Tower of the World Trade Center.
9:37 A.M.	Al-Qaeda hijackers crash a third plane into the Pentagon near Washington, DC.
9:42 A.M.	The US government orders all planes in the United States to land.
9:59 A.M.	The South Tower collapses.
10:03 A.M.	Al-Qaeda hijackers crash a fourth plane into a field in Pennsylvania.
10:28 A.M.	The North Tower collapses.
8:30 P.M.	President George W. Bush gives a speech to the nation.

COMPREHENSION QUESTIONS

Write your answers on a separate piece of paper.

1. Write a paragraph that explains the main ideas of Chapter 2.

2. Do you think the United States should have invaded Afghanistan after the attacks? Why or why not?

3. Where did al-Qaeda form?

   A. Afghanistan
   B. Iraq
   C. United States

4. Which place did the hijackers strike first?

   A. the Pentagon
   B. the World Trade Center
   C. the US Capitol

5. What does **spewed** mean in this book?

*The crash caused a huge explosion. Smoke and flames **spewed** out of the building. Firefighters rushed to the scene.*

    A. drove a large truck
    B. held very still
    C. came out quickly

6. What does **influence** mean in this book?

*US businesses have a huge effect on other countries. Al-Qaeda did not approve of this Western **influence**.*

    A. the ability to affect others
    B. the ability to travel quickly
    C. the ability to earn money

Answer key on page 64.

GLOSSARY

economy
The system of goods, services, money, and jobs in a certain place.

first responders
People who help during emergencies. They include police officers, firefighters, paramedics, and more.

hate crimes
Acts of violence that target and hurt members of a certain group, often based on skin color, religion, or sexuality.

hijackers
People who take over a vehicle illegally, usually by force.

invaded
Entered a place using force.

memorial
A structure built to remind people of a specific person or event.

militant
Willing to use violence to reach goals.

warrant
An order from a judge that allows a person to do something. Examples include arresting someone or searching a home.

Western
Having to do with countries in North America and Europe.

TO LEARN MORE
BOOKS

Manning, Matthew K. *Trakr Searches for Survivors: Heroic Police Dog of 9/11*. North Mankato, MN: Capstone Press, 2024.

Maranville, Amy. *The 9/11 Terrorist Attacks: A Day That Changed America*. North Mankato, MN: Capstone Publishing, 2022.

Rusick, Jessica. *September 11, 2001: Then and Now*. Minneapolis: Abdo Publishing, 2021.

ONLINE RESOURCES

Visit **www.apexeditions.com** to find links and resources related to this title.

ABOUT THE AUTHOR

Nick Rebman is a writer and editor who lives in Minnesota.

INDEX

ANSWER KEY:
1. Answers will vary; 2. Answers will vary; 3. A; 4. B; 5. C; 6. A